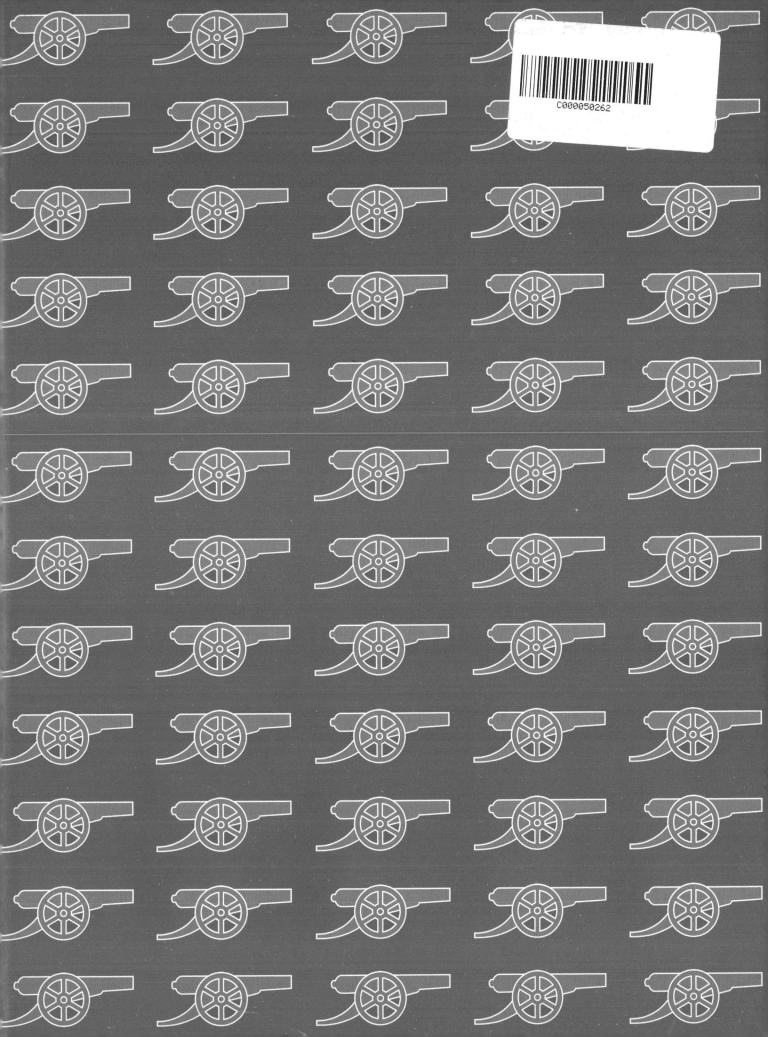

This is a Carlton book

First published in 2004 by Carlton Books Limited
20 Mortimer Street
London W1T 3JW

Arsenal.com

A CIP catalogue record of this book is
available from the British Library

ISBN 1 84442 611 4

Executive Editor: Roland Hall
Project Art Director: Darren Jordan
Design: Ben Ruocco
Picture Research: Stephen O'Kelly
Production: Lisa French
Gunnersaurus illustration p50–51: Des Taylor

Printed in Italy

Picture Acknowledgements
Colorsport: 44t, 44b, 45tr, 45bl.
Empics: 22l; /Barry Bland: 45tr; /S&G/ALPHA: 22m, 23;
/Barretts/ALPHA: 45br; /Peter Robinson: 22r, 39r.
All other pictures kindly supplied by **Arsenal Football Club:**
photographers **Stuart MacFarlane** & **David Price**

The Official
Arsenal
Annual 2005

Chas Newkey-Burden

CARLTON
BOOKS

Contents

"Everyone at Arsenal is extremely proud of last season's achievements. I dreamt and believed that we could win not just the Championship, but do so without losing a League match. The longer the season went on, the more I believed.

Of the three League titles we have won since I joined Arsenal, this was the most satisfying. It was definitely a season to remember forever, so I hope you enjoy the memories of it in this Annual.

Let's not forget some of the great performances we delivered in the cup competitions and the achievement of some of our younger players, who will hopefully become star names very soon.

Lastly, the fans played an important part in our success all season and on behalf of the players and myself, I'd like to thank you all for your support. We will be making every effort to build on this success in the future. But in the meantime, enjoy The Official Arsenal Annual 2005.

Thank you for your support,
Arsène Wenger, Manager

THE JUNIOR GUNNERS started way back in 1983 – over 21 years ago. Back then there were just 300 members. We reached an all-time high of 20,000 members not so long ago. It's not difficult to see why. There are lots of competitions and events all year, with great prizes like attending the JGs' Christmas party with the players! Members receive a fantastic souvenir pack, and they also automatically have the chance to be a mascot at a match during the season. All JGs also have access to reduced price tickets for first-team matches subject to availability, and get to take part in loads of events, competitions and quizzes held throughout the season including the Junior Gunners awards.

ARSENAL CAPTAIN PATRICK VIEIRA SAYS:
"The Junior Gunners is a great to way make new friends, and of course a good way to show support for Arsenal, plus there are lots of fun events to attend throughout the season."

If you are not already a Junior Gunner member, then why not give the Junior Gunners office a call on 020 7704 4160 and they will send you a membership form. Or you can look them up on the Arsenal website: www.arsenal.com or e-mail them at juniorgunners@arsenal.co.uk

Let the Scoring
Commence: We're off!

THE RECORD-BREAKING

SEASON

Arsenal's rivals seriously strengthened their squads over the summer, so something special was needed if the Gunners were to recapture the Premiership trophy. At the end of a breathtaking, dramatic campaign the trophy was safely back in the Highbury trophy cabinet. Not only that, all season Arsène Wenger's team set and broke record after record. So sit back and enjoy reliving the drama of a memorable Premiership season...

August 2003

Arsenal began the new season in winning style during an eventful meeting with Everton at Highbury. Enjoying plenty of possession, the Gunners kept visiting goalkeeper Richard Wright busy but the former Arsenal man could do nothing to stop Thierry Henry's first-half penalty nor Robert Pires' second-half strike. Both Sol Campbell and Everton's Li Tie were shown red cards, but Arsenal held out for a winning start to the campaign.

The Riverside is a happy hunting ground for Arsenal, who have won seven of their last eight League visits there, and they cruised to an emphatic 4–0 victory there. The game was all but over when Sylvain Wiltord put the visitors 3–0 ahead after Henry and Gilberto Silva had found the net. Wiltord netted again on the hour to put Arsenal where they spent so much of the season – at the top of the League!

Back at Highbury, Sol Campbell, who had played his 100th game for Arsenal at the Riverside, broke down a determined Aston Villa with a second-half header. Thierry Henry guaranteed the win in the 90th minute. Starring at the back as the Gunners kept a clean sheet was Kolo Touré, already proving to be an effective centre-back.

Arsenal overcame the misfortune of a bizarre tenth-minute own goal from Lauren to win 2–1 away to Manchester City. Goals from Sylvain Wiltord and Freddie Ljungberg wrapped up a highly successful August for Arsène Wenger's men in which they won four out of four Premiership matches, giving them the perfect start to the season.

AUGUST 16, 2003 ARSENAL 2–1 EVERTON
(HENRY 35 PEN, PIRES 58)
AUGUST 24, 2003 MIDDLESBROUGH 0–4
(HENRY 5, GILBERTO 13, WILTORD 22, 60)
AUGUST 27, 2003 ARSENAL 2–0 ASTON VILLA
(CAMPBELL 57, HENRY 90)
AUGUST 31, 2003 MANCHESTER CITY 1–2 ARSENAL
(WILTORD 47, LJUNGBERG 71)

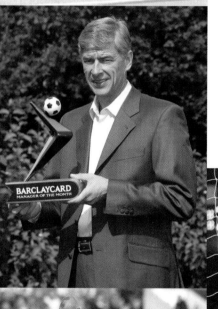

SEPTEMBER 13, 2003 ARSENAL 1–1 PORTSMOUTH
(HENRY 40 PEN)
SEPETMBER 21, 2003 MANCHESTER UNITED 0–0 ARSENAL
SEPTEMBER 26, 2003 ARSENAL 3–2 NEWCASTLE UNITED
(HENRY 18, 79 PEN, GILBERTO 67)

September 2003

Arsène Wenger was presented with the Manager of the Month award for August before the game against Portsmouth and Arsenal remained unbeaten at the end of the afternoon. Nine of the thirteen Arsenal players featured against Pompey had been involved in international duty the previous week and this showed in the 1–1 draw. Thierry Henry's twice taken penalty securing a point after Teddy Sheringham had put the visitors ahead.

After the mid-week Champions League disappointment against Inter Milan, a solid performance was required against the reigning champions Manchester United at Old Trafford – and that's exactly what Arsenal delivered. Ashley Cole hit the post with a rasping shot and Freddie Ljungberg also came close. Gunners fans cheered loudest when Ruud van Nistelrooy blasted a penalty against the crossbar right at the end of a tense match. The 0–0 draw earned Arsenal a point and at the end of a tough week, the team remained at the top of the table.

Friday night football came to Highbury and a five-goal thriller saw Arsenal emerge as 3–2 winners over Newcastle United and go four points clear at the top of the Premiership table. Gilberto scored his first goal at Highbury and the ever-prolific Thierry Henry netted twice to tie up a good night's work and another successful month in the Premiership for Arsenal.

... ARSENE'S AWARD ... THIERRY TOPS THE TOON ... RUUD PAYS THE PENALTY ...

9

October 2003

Beating Liverpool at Anfield is always a special result. But with young Frenchman Jérémie Aliadière's impressive full League debut, an assured performance in midfield from Edu in place of the injured Patrick Vieira and a stunning 25-yard curler from Robert Pires, there was much for Arsenal fans to celebrate as they watched the boys beat Liverpool 2–1. To top it off, this was the Gunners' seventh match without defeat against Liverpool.

Both Arsenal and Chelsea were unbeaten in the League going into the match at Highbury and only the Gunners emerged with that record intact. Edu gave Arsenal a fourth-minute league before Hernan Crespo's almost immediate equaliser. Henry capitalised on Carlo Cudicini's fumbling of a cross to secure the 2–1 victory that inflicted the first dent in Chelsea's hopes of winning the title.

Charlton Athletic's impressive form surprised people throughout the season and Arsenal's point at The

OCTOBER 4, 2003 LIVERPOOL 1–2 ARSENAL
(HYYPIA 31 (OG) PIRES 68)
OCTOBER 18, 2003 ARSENAL 2–1 CHELSEA
(EDU 5 HENRY 75)
OCTOBER 26, 2003 CHARLTON ATHLETIC 1–1 ARSENAL
(HENRY 39)

Valley was more than respectable. Thierry Henry's inch-perfect free-kick secured a point after Paolo Di Canio had put the Addicks ahead from the penalty spot. Arsenal ended the month at the top of the League, having won 24 out of a possible 30 League points and still unbeaten in the Premiership – perhaps the most competitive league on the planet.

Eduuuuuuuuuuuu!: Arsenal go one up against Chelsea.

Mad For It: Pires scores against Liverpool.

November 2003

In a text-book display of counter-attacking football, Arsenal swept aside a beleaguered Leeds United with a Thierry Henry brace among their goals in an impressive 4–1 victory. Still without captain Patrick Vieira, the Gunners displayed the depth in their squad by punishing Leeds' defensive frailties to the full. Gilberto and Pires also chipped in with a goal apiece to crown another impressive away victory.

Poor old Spurs had not won at Highbury for eleven seasons going into the first North London derby of the season. They must have believed they were on course to end that barren run when

Darren Anderton put them ahead after just five minutes at Highbury. So imagine their disappointment when second-half goals from Pires and Ljungberg sent them back across North London empty-handed once again. Kanu made his first Premiership start of the season in the derby victory.

In a season where Arsenal made setting and breaking records a habit, they set a Premiership record of 13 matches unbeaten since the start of the season with a 3–0 victory away to Birmingham City. A depleted team saw Pascal Cygan, Gael Clichy and Edu underline once again the depth in Arsène Wenger's squad. Ljungberg, Bergkamp and Pires were on target in Wenger's 400th match in charge of Arsenal.

Arsenal grabbed a hard-earned point at home to Fulham on the final day of the month after Cottagers goalkeeper Edwin van der Sar proved unbeatable in goal for the visitors despite Arsenal creating a hatful of chances.

NOVEMBER 1, 2003 LEEDS UNITED 1–4 ARSENAL
(HENRY 8, 33, PIRES 17, GILBERTO 50)
NOVEMBER 8, 2003 ARSENAL 2–1 TOTTENHAM HOTSPUR
(PIRES 69, LJUNGBERG 79)
NOVEMBER 22, 2003 BIRMINGHAM CITY 0–3 ARSENAL
(LJUNGBERG 4, BERGKAMP 80, PIRES 88)
NOVEMBER 30, 2003 ARSENAL 0–0 FULHAM

December 2003

Missing both Henry and Vieira, Arsenal seemed assured of a hard-earned victory at the Walkers Stadium until Craig Hignett's last-minute equaliser for Leicester City. Gilberto scored his fourth Premiership goal of the season and Arsenal's draw stretched their unbeaten Premiership run to 15 matches.

The longer the season went on, the more people sat up and took notice of Kolo Touré, and the Ivory Coast international was crucial at both ends of the field as Arsenal beat Blackburn Rovers 1–0 to return to the top of the League. Touré set up Bergkamp's winner and frustrated the Blackburn attack to help the Gunners keep another clean sheet.

After the disappointment of their visit to The Reebok Stadium at the climax of last season, Arsenal were determined not to leave the home of Bolton Wanderers empty-handed. The home team fought hard and disrupted Arsenal's strategy but the Gunners restored some pride with a 1–1 draw.

Wolves arrived at Highbury on Boxing Day desperate for points to take them off the bottom of the table. Despite a committed performance from the visitors, Arsenal cruised home to win 3–0, with Henry scoring twice. And Henry put in a vintage performance away to Southampton three days later, but just as in last season's FA Cup Final, it was Robert Pires who scored in Arsenal's 1–0 victory, which put them within a point of leaders Manchester United going into the New Year.

DECEMBER 6, 2003 LEICESTER CITY 1–1 ARSENAL
(GILBERTO 60)
DECEMBER 14, 2003 ARSENAL 1–0 BLACKBURN ROVERS
(BERGKAMP 11)
DECEMBER 20, 2003 BOLTON WANDERERS 1–1 ARSENAL
(PIRES 57)
DECEMBER 26, 2003 ARSENAL 3–0 WOLVERHAMPTON WANDERERS
(CRADDOCK OG 13, HENRY 20, 89)
DECEMBER 29, 2003
SOUTHAMPTON 0–1 ARSENAL
(PIRES 35)

Go Go Gilberto: A leaping header puts Arsenal ahead against Leicester City.

January 2004

Kanu scored his first Premiership goal of the season at Goodison Park against Everton but that was not enough to win the match as Tomas Radzinski equalised with 15 minutes to go. What was really needed was a comprehensive victory to answer the critics who were beginning to write off Arsenal's title chances.

And that's exactly what occurred against Middlesbrough. A sequence of four matches against the Riversiders in three different competitions began in the Premiership with Arsenal putting four past Steve McClaren's men for the second time this season. Ljungberg, Pires and Henry were among the scorers in an awesome display which left plenty for their opponents to ponder as they awaited their meeting in the FA Cup.

And so to Villa Park. Thierry Henry's pace on the ball is legendary, but he showed he has a quick mind as well as quick feet when he cheekily side-footed home a free-kick as the Aston Villa team were still preparing their wall. Henry added a second goal from the penalty spot in the second half and with news that Manchester United had lost at Wolves, the team could celebrate a two-point lead at the top of the table.

Touré's Away: Kolo's off to set one up for Bergkamp against Blackburn Rovers.

JANUARY 7, 2004 EVERTON 1–1 ARSENAL
(KANU 29)
JANUARY 10, 2004 ARSENAL 4–1 MIDDLESBROUGH
(HENRY 38 PEN, QUEUDRUE OG 45,
PIRES 57, LJUNGBERG 68)
JANUARY 18, 2004 ASTON VILLA 0–2 ARSENAL
(HENRY 29, 53 PEN)

Glovely Goal: Kanu and Cole celebrate.

FEBRUARY 1, 2004 ARSENAL 2–1
MANCHESTER CITY
(TARNAT 39 OG, HENRY 83)
FEBRUARY 7, 2004 WOLVERHAMPTON
WANDERERS 1–3 ARSENAL
(BERGKAMP 9, HENRY 58, TOURE 63)
FEBRUARY 10, 2004 ARSENAL 2–0 SOUTHAMPTON
(HENRY 31, 90)
FEBRUARY 21, 2004 CHELSEA 1–2 ARSENAL
(VIEIRA 15, EDU 21)
FEBRUARY 28, ARSENAL 2–1
CHARLTON ATHLETIC
(PIRES 2, HENRY 4)

ARS

February 2004

The signing of Jose Antonio Reyes had grabbed the headlines going into the home match against Manchester City, and although he nearly scored after replacing Bergkamp late on, it was Thierry Henry who starred in this match, firing the winner past David James in goal. James's predecessor, Arsenal legend David Seaman, was given a standing ovation by the whole ground at the beginning of the afternoon.

Another record was set by Arsenal when they beat Wolves 3–1 at Molineux – this time a club record of 24 games unbeaten since the start of the season. Bergkamp got the first and was joined by Henry and Touré on the scoresheet in a game memorable for excellent creative play from Pires.

Thierry Henry scored his 100th Premiership goal and Arsenal went five points clear at the top of the table after their 2–0 victory over Southampton. Reyes made his full debut for Arsenal in this match and continued to impress, but it was Henry with two goals who won the plaudits as he reached his Premiership century.

Having seen off Chelsea in the FA Cup the previous weekend, Arsenal repeated the 2–1 scoreline of that tie when the two sides met at Stamford Bridge in the League. Gudjohnsen gave Chelsea the lead in the first minute but Arsenal battled back with goals from Vieira and Edu, once more breaking the hearts of Chelsea fans.

Arsenal's magic touch in London derbies continued when they beat Charlton Athletic 2–1 at Highbury, with Pires and Henry's goals coming in a really exciting opening four minutes. Despite a second-half goal from Charlton's Claus Jensen, Arsenal held out professionally for the win.

March 2004

The longer the season went on, the higher the stakes became, as critics predicted that Arsenal's fine Premiership form would collapse as they reached the final hurdles. Any critics hoping that successive games against Blackburn Rovers and Bolton Wanderers would herald a repeat of two disappointing results during last season's run-in were underestimating Arsenal's resolve in this fantastic campaign.

Goals from Henry and Pires sealed the three points at Ewood Park. Then Arsenal equalled the English top-flight record of starting a season unbeaten in 29 games when they beat Bolton 2–1 at Highbury.

Pires was again on the scoresheet and was joined there by Bergkamp in an enjoyable afternoon of football. Having equalled that record, Arsenal beat it the following weekend in a 1–1 draw with Manchester United.

Although disappointed not to win all three points, Arsène Wenger was certainly well satisfied with another point gained. Henry put Arsenal ahead with a sublime, swerving shot, which looked set to be the winner until substitute Louis Saha equalised in the final stages.

At the end of March, Arsenal stood 12 points ahead of Manchester United and were widely tipped to be Champions elect. But Wenger's team were too professional to let the hype go to their heads and continued to let their football do the talking...

Score More: Thierry's wonder-goal against Manchester United.

MARCH 13, 2004 BLACKBURN ROVERS 0–2 ARSENAL
(HENRY 57, PIRES 87)
MARCH 20, 2004 ARSENAL 2–1 BOLTON WANDERERS
(PIRES 16, BERGKAMP 24)
MARCH 28, 2004 ARSENAL 1–1 MANCHESTER UNITED
(HENRY 50)

2–1 down, 4–2 up. It was a very Good Friday at Highbury Stadium.

April 2004

A solid, winning performance was needed when Liverpool visited Highbury on Good Friday. So when Arsenal were 2–1 down at half-time, it was clear that something special had to happen in the second half. The Gunners, and particularly Thierry Henry, returned for the second half like men on a mission. Before all the fans had even returned to their seats, a Pires strike and Henry wonder goal had put Arsenal ahead. Henry completed his hat-trick after 78 minutes and Highbury was awash with joy and relief. Arsenal continued their unbeaten run

APRIL 9, 2004 ARSENAL 4–2 LIVERPOOL
(HENRY 31, 50, 78, PIRES 49)
APRIL 11, 2004 NEWCASTLE UNITED 0–0 ARSENAL
APRIL 16, 2004 ARSENAL 5–0 LEEDS UNITED
(PIRES 6, HENRY 27, 33 PEN, 50, 67)
APRIL 25, 2004 TOTTENHAM HOTSPUR 2–2
(VIEIRA 3, PIRES 35)

and extended their lead at the top of the table with a professionally-earned 0–0 draw away to Newcastle United. Playing their fourth game in eight days, Arsenal had good chances to score through Sylvain Wiltord, Henry and Touré but had to settle for a point against a determined Newcastle side. Jens Lehmann impressed with a spectacular save to deny Craig Bellamy.

When Leeds United came to Highbury for a Friday night match, they might have wondered how they would contain the Arsenal attack, and particularly Henry. They would have left asking the same question after the striker netted four goals in a spectacular 5–0 victory. Henry's fourth was particularly impressive, seeing

him race from the halfway line and take on the heart of the Leeds defence before slotting home.

And so to White Hart Lane where Arsenal needed only a point to be crowned Premiership Champions. Having won the League at Old Trafford in 2002, to win it at the ground of Arsenal's local rivals, Tottenham Hotspur, would be a sweet moment for the players and fans alike. Patrick Vieira and Robert Pires put Arsenal ahead but a spirited fightback from Spurs meant the travelling fans could not relax until the final whistle. Jubilant but dignified celebrations from the Arsenal players and fans followed the match. Arsenal – the worthiest of Champions!

May 2004

With the Championship secured, Arsenal set out to make history by remaining unbeaten until the end of the Premiership season. First up, Birmingham City came to Highbury and the Gunners put in a professional performance that earned a point and kept the unbeaten run going. Martin Keown made a late appearance as a substitute as he chased enough appearances to secure a much-deserved Championship medal.

Arsène Wenger gave youngster David Bentley a run-out at Fratton Park, and along with the rest of the Arsenal team, Bentley performed well. After the team went one goal down in the first half, the unbeaten record looked under threat. But never underestimate the character of this Gunners side. Jose Antonio Reyes fired a second-half equaliser to secure a point. And who was that substitute sent on in the final minute? Oh yes, Martin Keown.

Reyes was on the scoresheet again at Loftus Road as the Gunners overcame a resilient Fulham side to put themselves within touching distance of completing the season unbeaten. In the final game of the season, former Gunner Paul Dickov threatened to ruin the party by putting Leicester City ahead. But goals from Henry and Vieira secured the victory and made history for Arsenal as they completed the Premiership season unbeaten.

After the match, the team were presented with the Premiership trophy and celebrated in style in front of their loyal fans. Awesome, invincible, immortal – you just cannot beat Arsenal.

MAY 1, 2004 ARSENAL 0–0 BIRMINGHAM CITY
MAY 4, 2004 PORTSMOUTH 1–1 ARSENAL
(REYES 50)
MAY 9, 2004 FULHAM 0–1 ARSENAL
(REYES 9)
MAY 15, 2004 ARSENAL 2–1 LEICESTER CITY
(HENRY 47 PEN, VIEIRA 66)

Far left: Reyes nets a goal against Portsmouth.
Below left: Vieira scores against Leicester City.
Left: The Captain's Cup!

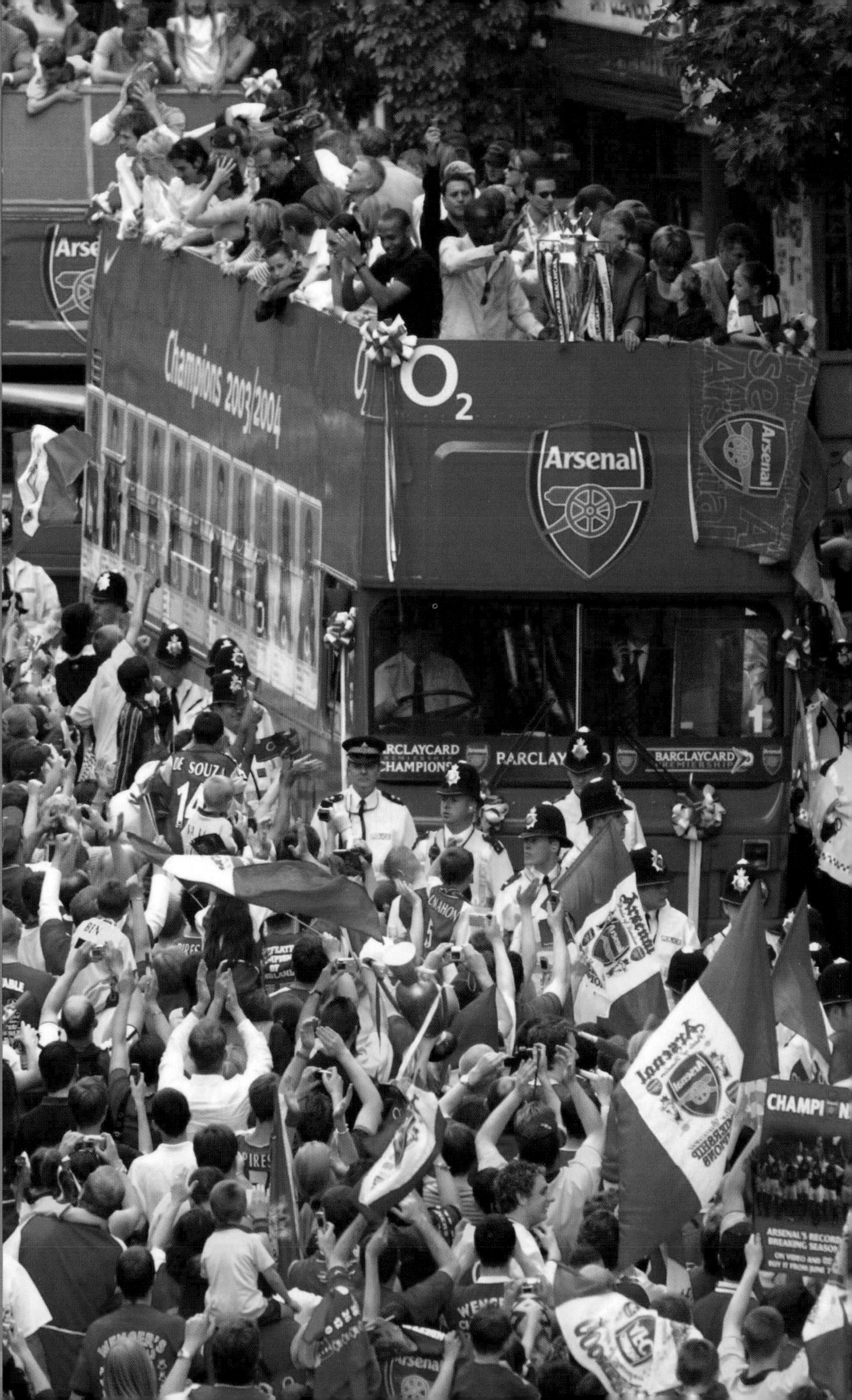
Champions 2003/2004
O2
Arsenal
BARCLAYCARD
CHAMPIONS

Unbeatable!

You'll Never Beat The Arsenal!
In an historic Premiership campaign, Arsenal were simply the best. Over 38 league games, not a single opponent managed to beat a team with perhaps the most effective, attractive and exciting style of play ever witnessed on planet football.

A solid back four, an awesome midfield unit and the greatest attackers in the League, spearheaded by the unstoppable Thierry Henry, Arsenal treated fans across the country to breathtaking football all season.

The longer the season went on, the more records were broken and the better the team's performances became – even once the Championship was secured, Arsenal remained one hundred per cent focused on completing the campaign in style.

This team and their manager will go down in history for their achievement of going the whole season unbeaten. It was a season that will be remembered for ever.

Is there a player on the planet performing better than Thierry Henry right now? An admiring public almost ran out of words to describe the dazzling, lightning-fast play of Thierry last season as the goal machine fired Arsenal to the title.

The Lowdown: It's difficult to believe that Thierry Henry arrived at Highbury as a winger after Arsène Wenger swooped to buy him from Juventus. Moved into a central striking position, Thierry has never looked back as he scores goals and performs moves that take supporters' breath away. His pace takes the breath away too – that of opposition defenders! Thierry's collection of individual honours since he joined Arsenal include Golden Boots, PFA Player of the Year awards and two Premiership Goal of the Season gongs.

During the 2003–04 title-winning season, Thierry was more prolific than ever and scored in even the biggest games. His goals included a pair of hat-tricks against Liverpool and Newcastle, two at the San Siro against Inter Milan, a memorable, swerving netbuster at home to Manchester United and let's not forget four goals in one game against Leeds United.

Arsenal fans turn up to Highbury week after week knowing that when they are watching Thierry Henry, they are watching a player of extraordinary talent at the top of his game. Thierry is simply the best and opponents found him absolutely unstoppable as Arsenal won the 2003–04 Premiership title.

Patrick Vieira says:
"I definitely think Thierry is the best player in the world. No striker works so hard, scores the goals and creates the goals. He is the best."

Season highlight:
His spectacular hat-trick against Liverpool – the perfect tonic at the end of a tough week.

Thierry Henry

Arsène Wenger says:
"I think every Arsenal supporter is totally convinced by Theirry. Slowly you have seen from year to year that his reputation has grown and what we have all sensed for a long time at the Club about how far he can go is now becoming obvious for everybody in the world."

NAME	THIERRY HENRY
BORN	AUGUST 17, 1977 PARIS, FRANCE
POSITION	STRIKER
HEIGHT	188CM
WEIGHT	83KG
PREVIOUS CLUBS	AS MONACO (FRA), JUVENTUS (ITA)

Arsenal's successful captain is an awesome talent who is without doubt one of the greatest midfielders in the world. Leading by example, the skipper was his usual dynamic, dependable self in 2003–04 season.

PATRICK VIEIRA	NAME
JUNE 28, 1976 DAKAR, SENEGAL	BORN
MIDFIELDER	POSITION
193CM	HEIGHT
83KG	WEIGHT
CANNES (FRA), AC MILAN (ITA)	PREVIOUS CLUBS

Patrick Vieira

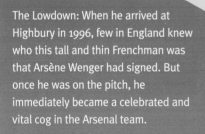

The Lowdown: When he arrived at Highbury in 1996, few in England knew who this tall and thin Frenchman was that Arsène Wenger had signed. But once he was on the pitch, he immediately became a celebrated and vital cog in the Arsenal team.

The Frenchman is a testament to the genius of Wenger's management. Arsène Wenger was one of the only people in the game to identify the potential of a player that few people knew about even if he had been bought from AC Milan! And how Patrick has rewarded Wenger's faith! The winner of three League Championships and a hat-trick of FA Cups, Patrick is a powerful tackler, an athletic dribbler and incisive passer of the ball.

Admired hugely by his fellow professionals, Patrick is the first player to be voted into the PFA Premier League Team of the Year by his fellow professionals for five consecutive years. He has also won the World Cup and European Championship with France. Is there anything Patrick hasn't got? Ah yes, the Champions League – a trophy captain Patrick is desperate to lift. Watch this space!

Arsène Wenger says:
"Patrick is the captain because he is a natural leader. He is physically very strong and can control the game from the midfield."

Season highlight:
Scoring the opener at White Hart Lane as Arsenal won the title!

Patrick Vieira says:
"I am proud to be the captain of the team. Everybody gives their best and, when we are on the pitch, nobody tries to cheat. They just do the best for each other. In the dressing room the atmosphere is fantastic."

The History

Listen up at the back! Today in class we are studying the history of Arsenal. We'll find out how some factory workers in South London created the team that went onto become one of the greatest names in the history of world football.

Early Days

The Club was formed in 1886 by a group of workers at a Woolwich armaments factory in South London – at this point the Club was known as Dial Square. It then became known as Royal Arsenal, then Woolwich Arsenal, before becoming Arsenal Football Club. Arsenal was elected to the Second Division of the football league in 1893, then the First Division in 1904. In 1913, the Club moved to Highbury Stadium. In 1925, Herbert Chapman was appointed manager and over the following nine years, he transformed the Club into one of the greatest in world history.

Arsenal won three League titles and two FA Cup under Chapman, who also introduced white sleeves to the Arsenal shirts, had the local underground station renamed after the Club and also pioneered the use of shirt numbers. A bust of Herbert Chapman sits in the reception of the East Stand of Arsenal Stadium as a reminding testament.

Doing the Double

Two further League titles and an FA Cup followed in the late 1940s and early 1950s but the Gunners didn't win another trophy until the UEFA Cup in 1970 by beating Belgian club Anderlecht. The 1970–1971 season saw Arsenal win the League and Cup Double, securing the League title at White Hart Lane and beating Liverpool in the FA Cup with a goal from Charlie George.

Later that decade, Arsenal reached three successive FA Cup Finals, winning the middle one in 1979 3–2 against Manchester United in a thrilling match that became known as the 'five-minute Final'. One of Arsenal's greatest ever players, Liam Brady, took part in that match.

The Modern Era

George Graham, who had played in the 1971 Double-winning side, took over as manager in 1986 and won two League titles, two League Cups, one FA Cup and the European Cup Winners' Cup with the Gunners. Most famous of these wins were the 1989 League title (secured with a dramatic last-minute Michael Thomas goal at Anfield), the unique 'Cup Double' of 1993 (when Arsenal beat Sheffield Wednesday in both the FA Cup and League Cup Finals) and the famous "1–0 to the Arsenal" European Cup Winners' Cup Final victory over Parma in 1994. A key player in Arsenal history and the Club's greatest ever goalscorer, Ian Wright, was a star of the George Graham era, alongside legendary captain Tony Adams.

Arsène Wenger became manager in 1996 and the team won the League and Cup double in 1998 at the end of his first full season in charge. Playing scintillating football, they repeated this feat in 2002, beating Chelsea in the Cup Final. In 2003, they won the FA Cup again, after reaching the Final for the third successive year, and then in 2004, Wenger's Wonderlads won the Premiership trophy after going the whole season unbeaten...

Above left: The legendary Herbert Chapman.
Above centre: Chapman's 1938 team showing off some silverware.
Above right: Charlie George and Frank McLintock with the FA Cup in 1979 – the year Arsenal won the Double for the first time.
Right: Charlie George at Highbury.

COUNTRY ITALY

CITY MILAN

RESULT INTER MILAN 1–5 ARSENAL

DATE TUESDAY NOVEMBER 25, 2003

Player's Postcard:
We had a great night in the San Siro. The pressure was on us to get a good result after the disappointing game against Inter at Highbury.
We won 5–1 – Thierry got two goals and Robert, Edu and Freddie also scored. Thierry, Dennis and Kanu had all played in this stadium before when they played in Italy but none of them remember a match as great as this one. Wish you were here!

"We're all going on a European tour" sang the Arsenal fans last season during the Club's equal finest showing in the Champions League to date. It proved to be an amazing tour around Europe that saw the travelling Arsenal fans follow the team to places like chilly Russia in the north and Spain in the south. And remember those amazing victories against Inter Milan and Celta Vigo? Re-live a great European campaign and plot the team's progress around the continent with our map of Europe...

COUNTRY SPAIN

CITY VIGO

RESULT CELTA VIGO 2–3 ARSENAL

DATE TUESDAY FEBRUARY 24, 2004

Player's postcard:
We'd never won a game in the Champions League in Spain so we were determined to get a result here. But little did we know the game would be such a thriller! Edu got two goals and Robert scored the winner after Celta had fought their way back into the game. We're now very hopeful of reaching the Quarter-Finals.

RUSSIA	COUNTRY
MOSCOW	CITY
LOCOMOTIV MOSCOW 0—0 ARSENAL	RESULT
TUESDAY SEPTEMBER 30, 2003	DATE

Player's postcard:

After a long trip, we arrived in Moscow without Freddie, Patrick, Dennis or Sol. Edu and Ray came in and we battled to a respectable draw in front of 30,000 fans. Thierry and Robert came close to scoring and though we would have liked to have won, another point on the board was very welcome. Thanks to the fans who made such a long trip to support us!

UKRAINE	COUNTRY
KIEV	CITY
DYNAMO KIEV 2—1 ARSENAL	RESULT
TUESDAY OCTOBER 21, 2003	DATE

Player's postcard:

What a stadium! Over 80,000 fans came to watch our match here, we only wish we could have won in front of them. After another long trip, we had a real battle on our hands to take anything from this game against very organised opponents. Thierry scored a great goal ten minutes from time but we were not able to build on it.

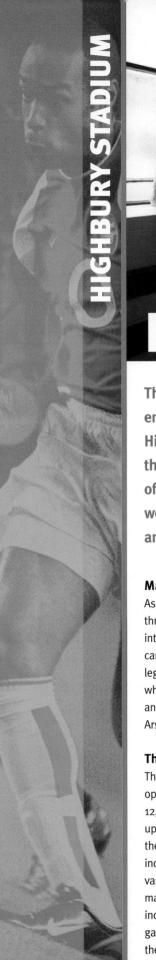

Highbury

There's no place like home and Arsenal fans, players and employees alike have grown enormously attached to Highbury since the Club moved there in 1913. Over the years, the stadium has changed to keep up and be at the forefront of modern developments but has also retained its charm. As we approach the end of the Club's time here, let's take a tour around the famous stadium.

Marble Halls

As soon as you enter Arsenal Stadium through the main entrance, you step into the famed Marble Halls and you can see the black marble bust of legendary manager Herbert Chapman, who won three League championships and the FA Cup when he managed Arsenal in the 1920s and 1930s.

The North Bank Stand

The new North Bank Stand was opened in 1993, accommodating 12,400 supporters on two tiers (4,000 upper and 8,400 lower). It has some of the best facilities in world football, including a merchandise shop, a variety of superb catering points and matchday entertainment that includes live bands and arcade games. The North Bank also houses the Arsenal Museum...

The Arsenal Museum

The Museum opened in October 1993 and has had a flood of thrilled visitors ever since. Situated on the second floor of the North Bank Stand, it is the largest, most extensive archive of a single club's football memorabilia in Britain. It includes, amongst other exhibits, waxworks of Gunners stars, shirts and balls used in legendary Arsenal matches and the bus which Arsenal use to parade their trophies around Islington.

The Clock End

The South Stand or Clock End now holds 7,000 seats and 53 luxury boxes. The clock on top of the stand has told the time for Arsenal fans for many decades.

HERBERT
CHAPMAN

Dressing Rooms

Where the players prepare for and wind down from matches. With under-floor heating and extensive physiotherapy facilities, the players could not be better prepared for action!

Jumbotron Screens

The stadium has two enormous jumbotron screens in the North West and South East corners of the ground. These keep fans entertained with excellent matchday entertainment including highlights of recent games, Manager Arsène Wenger announcing the line-up for each match 'as-live' and even instant replays of goals and key action.

A Famous Ground

The Highbury Stadium has featured in two films. *The Arsenal Stadium Mystery* was released in 1940 and was a murder mystery set in the ground. More recently, the film of Nick Hornby's book *Fever Pitch* also featured action in and outside the stadium.

The New Stadium...

Arsenal Football Club will kick off the 2006–07 season in a new home that is more than a world-class stadium. The £357m construction at Ashburton Grove will be state-of-the-art – a home fit for kings. Here are some key facts to give you a flavour of what will be our new home.

... a home fit for kings

- The site of the new stadium is 17 acres.

- It will have a capacity of 60,000 including 150 executive boxes and extensive hospitality facilities.

- A total of 1,000 construction employees are working on the new stadium.

- The height of the new stadium will be 46 metres from ground level to its highest point.

- There will be approximately 250 catering service points around the stadium.

- The pitch will be 113m by 76m. (Compared to 105m by 70m at Highbury).

- There will be 41 television camera positions throughout the stadium, as well as 215 seats for the media.

- The stadium will be the site for a new 1,000-square metre Arsenal megastore.

- There will be capacity for up to 250 wheelchair users at the new stadium. These positions will be provided at all public and corporate levels throughout the building.

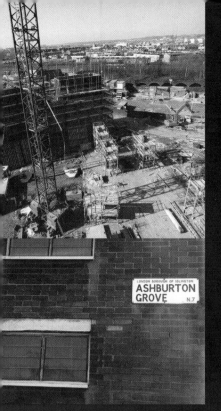

The Players' Verdict

Patrick Vieria:

"Moving to a new stadium is obviously a big change for the Club, after calling Highbury home for so long. I believe moving from Highbury is the right decision in order to progress. The new stadium will be impressive and will definitely be the envy of clubs, not only in England, but across the world."

Thierry Henry:

"If you want to move forward and be a bigger team in Europe, you need this kind of great stadium. And for the fans it will be lovely. A lot of my friends and a lot of people in London can't get tickets for Highbury, so it's great that many more supporters will be able to go to matches in the new stadium."

Ashley Cole:

"The new stadium should ensure that we can compete with the very biggest clubs in the Europe. Highbury is special to the fans of course, but also to the players, I'll certainly never forget the first time I played there. We'll all be sad to see it go but moving to a new stadium will be an exciting new chapter in the Club's long and proud history."

Top 10 Goals

The Gunners have fired wonder goal after wonder goal past opposition keepers across England and Europe this season. Here are the Top 10 super strikes from a vintage campaign...

10

Scorer: Thierry Henry
Match: Aston Villa 0–2 Arsenal
January 18, 2004 Premiership
The goal: Thierry's moment of cheeky genius as he quite rightly side-footed home a free-kick while Villa were still preparing their wall.

7

Scorer: David Bentley
Match: Arsenal 4–1 Middlesbrough
January 24, 2004 FA Cup
The goal: A glimpse of the future perhaps, as David Bentley chipped a great goal over Mark Schwarzer to cap another cup victory.

6

Scorer: Ashley Cole
Match: Arsenal 1–0 Dynamo Kiev
November 5, 2003 Champions League
The goal: Keeping his nerve, Ashley proved that top goals come from all over the field with this vital Euro strike.

3

Scorer: Patrick Vieria
Match: Tottenham Hotspur 2–2 Arsenal
April 24, 2004 Premiership
The goal: From a Spurs corner, Henry burst up the pitch, passed to Pires who crossed for the captain to score.

2

Scorer: Robert Pires
Match: Liverpool 1–2 Arsenal
October 2, 2003 Premiership
The goal: An unstoppable, curling 25-yard right-footer sealed the win at Anfield.

9

Scorer: Robert Pires
Match: Inter Milan 1–5 Arsenal
November 25, 2004 Champions
League
The goal: After fine work from
youngster Jérémie Aliadière,
Robert's strike capped an historic
performance.

8

Scorer: Thierry Henry
Match: Arsenal 1–1 Manchester Utd
March 28, 2004 Premiership
The goal: It's that man again!
This time it was a swerving long-
range shot that seemed bound for
the back of the net.

5

Scorer: Thierry Henry
Match: Arsenal 5–0 Leeds United
April 16, 2004 Premiership
The goal: Henry ran from the
halfway line taking on half the Leeds
team on his own. One of four goals
from the super striker in this match.

4

Scorer: Jose Antonio Reyes
Match: Arsenal 2–1 Chelsea
February 15, 2004 FA Cup
The goal: The first of two goals
from the Spaniard in this tie,
this 25-yard volley had the crowd
in raptures.

1

Scorer: Thierry Henry
Match: Arsenal 4–2 Liverpool
April 9, 2004 Premiership
The goal: A determined, mazy run
and a cool finish puts Arsenal's
season back on track.

Two on the trot: the Arsenal team celebrate their second consecutive FA Cup win. This one was against Southampton in 2003.

A remarkable run...

Arsenal fans are used to success in the FA Cup. Arsenal have won the famed cup nine times and three of those victories have come in the reign of Arsène Wenger. On January 5, 2002, Arsenal travelled to Vicarage Road to play Watford. Goals from Henry, Ljungberg, Kanu and Bergkamp gave the Gunners a 4–2 victory and a place in the Fourth Round of that season's FA Cup competition.

So began an amazing 18-match unbeaten run in the FA Cup that saw Arsenal score 48 goals, concede just 13, lift the FA Cup in two consecutive seasons, appear in two more Finals (having lost to Liverpool in 2001) and play some of the finest football the famous old competition has ever seen. So sit back and re-live some of the key highlights of this remarkable run...

ARSENAL 1–0 LIVERPOOL

2001–02 Fourth Round
January 27, 2002
Revenge was in the air at Highbury as holders Liverpool arrived. A first-half Dennis Bergkamp goal sealed victory for the Gunners as the previous season's disappointment against Liverpool in the Final at Cardiff was avenged.

ARSENAL 2–0 CHELSEA

2001–02 Final
May 4, 2002
As the Gunners reached touching distance of a memorable Double, great goals from Ljungberg and Parlour won the FA Cup for Arsenal. Patrick Vieira and Tony Adams jointly lifted the trophy as an old captain bowed out and a new one was crowned.

MAN UTD 0–2 ARSENAL

2002–03 Fifth Round
February 15 ,2003
All talk going into the match centred around Arsène Wenger's decision to leave Henry on the bench for this crucial clash with Arsenal's old rivals. A goal in each half from Edu and Wiltord put Arsenal in the Quarter-Finals and showed that the Gunners are far from a one-man show.

ARSENAL 1–0 SOUTHAMPTON

2002–03 Final
May 17, 2003
Arsenal, in their third consecutive Final, by this stage knew their way around the Millennium Stadium. Robert Pires certainly did as his goal meant the FA Cup stayed where it belonged – in the Highbury trophy cabinet! A fantastic team performance.

LEEDS UTD 1–4 ARSENAL

2003–04 Third Round
January 4, 2004
Hopes were high among home supporters when Mark Viduka gave Leeds the lead in the eighth minute, but goals from Henry, Edu, Pires and Touré (with his first goal of the season) gave Arsenal victory.

ARSENAL 2–1 CHELSEA

2003–04 Fifth Round
February 15, 2004
The match where José Antonio Reyes was formally crowned as the new king of Highbury! After Mutu had given Chelsea a first-half lead, Reyes cracked a 25-yard shot into the top right-hand corner of the net – and added a second five minutes later. Cue utter pandemonium in the crowd and a place in the next round...

MORE MAGIC MOMENTS

Going 2–0 up in the opening nine minutes of the 3–0 Sixth Round replay victory over Newcastle in 2002.

The Arsenal fans applauding Farnborough Town off the field after beating the team 5–1 in the 2003 Third Round.

David Seaman's wonder save as Arsenal beat Sheffield Utd in 2003.

Lauren's goal crowning a 3–1 victory over Chelsea in the 2003. Quarter-Final replay

David Bentley's chip against Middlesbrough in the 2004 Fourth Round.

Arsenal smashed their transfer record to bring Jose Antonio to Highbury and everything we've seen of the spectacular Spanish international so far shows what a great addition he is...

The Lowdown: Jose Antonio joined Seville at the age of nine and made his debut for the first team there at 16. He scored his first goal in a 3–2 win over Espanyol. At 20, he won his first international cap for Spain as they beat Portugal 3–0.

Widely regarded as the Spanish League's most exciting young talent, Jose Antonio was bought by Arsène Wenger in January 2004. His first great moment for Arsenal came in the FA Cup tie with Chelsea when he scored twice to win the tie 2–1 for the Gunners.

As with so many Wenger signings, he is very fast, so much so that the great Zinedine Zidane once said Jose Antonio "must have been on a motorbike" after he had helped Seville thrash the mighty Real Madrid 4–1.

The son of another talented player, Jose Antonio is now surrounded by some of the greatest footballers in the world at Highbury and after a successful, title-winning first few months at Arsenal, Jose is looking forward to his first full season at the Club.

The English translation of Reyes is 'kings' and Jose Antonio has every chance of becoming the new 'king of Highbury' for some years to come!

Season highlight:
His first goal for the Club – that spectacular left-foot screamer against Chelsea.

Arsène Wenger says:
"We watched him at least 30 to 40 times for Seville. We have done our homework. He has the qualities to suit our game because we want play based on technique and sharp movement – and he has that."

Jose Antonio Reyes

NAME	JOSE ANTONIO REYES
BORN	SEPTEMBER 1, 1983 UTRERA, SPAIN
POSITION	MIDFIELD/FORWARD
HEIGHT	175CM
WEIGHT	71KG
PREVIOUS CLUB	SEVILLE (SPA)

Jose Antonio says:
"I like the fact that here you are allowed to play more without the referee whistling. I enjoy this. It means games can become more intense and I think it gives me a chance to play better than I did in Spain."

French international Robert has won admirers across the world for his incisive attacking play at Highbury since he joined the Gunners in 2000. He's also won a medal or two along the way!

The Lowdown: In his first season for Arsenal (2000–01) Robert showed the dribbling ability, precise passing and excellent finishing we have since become accustomed to. The following season, Robert was the undoubted star of Arsenal's 2002 Double, even though he missed the very end of the run-in through injury. The following season he got 14 goals in 21 Premiership starts and won the FA Cup for Arsenal when he scored the winner against Southampton.

Robert has won respect for his exciting and professional approach to the game. This is seen in the numerous personal honours he has collected so far including being named the Football Writers' Player of the Year, twice featured in the Premiership Team of the Season and the Premier League Overseas Team of the Decade.

On the international stage, Robert has won the World Cup, European Championship and the Confederations Cup. This global champion was a key part of the Arsenal team that won the title again in 2004 and he is keen to add more winners' medals to his collection in the future!

Season highlight:
Scoring at White Hart Lane as Arsenal won the League!

His captain, Patrick Vieira, says:
"Robert is a very important player for us, he can set up and score lots of goals and he is absolutely vital to our success."

Arsène Wenger says:
"Robert is very talented and can change the game easily. He is definitely one of the greatest players I have ever managed."

Robert says:
"I love English football, it gives me reason to live. Every time I play, be it at Highbury or elsewhere, I get the same feeling. I love it. I would love to play in the new stadium! The chance to play in front of 60,000 spectators is a fantastic one."

Robert Pires

ROBERT PIRES	NAME
OCTOBER 29, 1973 IN REIMS, FRANCE	BORN
MIDFIELDER/FORWARD	POSITION
185CM	HEIGHT
74KG	WEIGHT
STADE DE REIMS, FC METZ, OLYMPIQUE MARSEILLE (ALL FRA)	PREVIOUS CLUBS

SONGS FROM THE HOME OF FOOTBALL

The fans have a part to play in the success of the team and there's no better way of doing that than by singing your hearts out at Highbury. Here are a few of the most popular tunes regularly sung at home.

**Suuuper Super Bob, Suuuper Super Bob
Suuuper Suuuper Bob, Super Robert Pires**

**Arsène Wenger's magic, He wears a magic hat
And when he saw the Championship
He said I'm having that!**

**We love you Freddie, 'cos you've got red hair
We love you Freddie, 'cos you're everywhere
We love you Freddie, you're Arsenal through and through...**

**There's only one Dennis Bergkamp,
One Dennis Bergkamp, Walking along singing a song
Walking in a Bergkamp wonderland**

**Vieira... ooh ooh ooh ooh, Vieira... ooh ooh ooh ooh
He comes from Senegal, He plays for Arsenal
Vieira... ooh ooh ooh ooh**

It's not just words and pictures that can tell a story – numbers can too. So here is a maths lesson with a difference...

43
The time in minutes it took Thierry Henry to complete his wonder hat-trick against Leeds United

6
The number of languages Arsène Wenger speaks

2,000
The number of new homes that will be built in Islington as a result of the Ashburton Grove project

9
The number of FA Cups Arsenal have won

8
The number of different nation-alities of Arsenal's goalscorers in the 2003–04 season

1,800
The number of calls ChildLine (Arsenal's Charity of the Season for 2003–2004) receives every day

Henry and Parlour's Big Night Out: Thierry and the team can't stop scoring against Inter!

12
The number of League Championships won by the Gunners

23
The number of television cameras at Highbury for live matches

3
The number of League titles won by Martin Keown during his Highbury career

181
The number of matches it took Thierry Henry to score 100 Arsenal goals

6
The number of National Premier League titles the Arsenal Ladies team have won

4
The number of Arsenal players who have won the World Cup

17
The total goals scored by Arsenal in the Champions' League of 2003–04

0
The number of people who saw Arsenal lose a Premiership game in the 2003–2004 season

1,060,444
Total attendance at Highbury for the Undefeated season 2003–04

ARSENAL QUIZ

Do you think you're an Arsenal expert? Then tackle this quiz to show you're the one with the knowledge!
Can you go through the whole quiz undefeated?

Scoring Scoring Arsenal

1 Thierry Henry, Dennis Bergkamp and Marc Overmars all scored their first Arsenal goals against which Premiership side?
2 Who scored twice when Arsenal beat Inter Milan 5–1 in the San Siro?
3 Which team did Jose Antonio Reyes score twice against in the FA Cup?
4 Which defender scored the winner against Dynamo Kiev last season?
5 David Bentley got his first goal against which team in the FA Cup in 2004?
6 Patrick Vieira scored his first goal this season against which side?
7 Who scored Arsenal's first goal of the Premiership campaign?
8 Arsenal scored four goals on three separate occasions against the same team last season. Name that team.
9 Who scored Arsenal's winner in the 3–2 away win over Celta Vigo?
10 Which player scored his 150th Arsenal goal against Leeds United?

Transfer time

11 Which Italian side did Thierry Henry join the Gunners from?
12 Which player did Arsenal loan to Barcelona in 2003–04?
13 Which Arsenal striker joined the club from Seville?
14 True or false: Robert Pires joined Arsenal from Paris St Germain.
15 What year did Sylvain Wiltord join Arsenal?
16 Which team did Jens Lehmann join Arsenal from?
17 Which team did Edu join the Gunners from?
18 Which team did Arsenal loan Jermaine Pennant to last season?
19 Which famous Spanish team did Arsenal sell two players to in the summer of 2000?
20 True or false: Gilberto signed for Arsenal from Porto.

Know your squad

21 Gael Clichy made his Premiership debut away to which Midlands team?
22 Ajax and which other side have Bergkamp and Kanu both played for?
23 In which country was Kolo Touré born?
24 In what season did Ashley Cole make his first-team debut for Arsenal?
25 Who wears the number 8 shirt at Arsenal?
26 What country was Lauren born in?
27 Which team did Freddie Ljungberg score his first goal against?
28 Which French side did Arsène Wenger win the Double with?
29 What nationality is Jérémie Aliadière?
30 Which Arsenal legend had his testimonial match in May 2004?

Cole's Goal: Just as you thought Arsenal would drop out of the Champions League, up popped Ash.

I want to give my best
for my

Big European Night: Thierry helped Arsenal inflict one of the worst home defeats of all time against Inter of Milan.

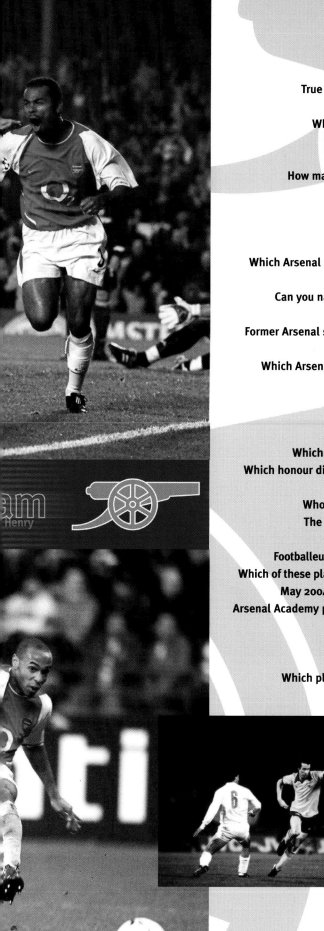

International time

Fun facts

Arsenal and Ireland star Liam Brady was no stranger to Europe: here he's playing Valencia in the European Cup Winners' Cup.

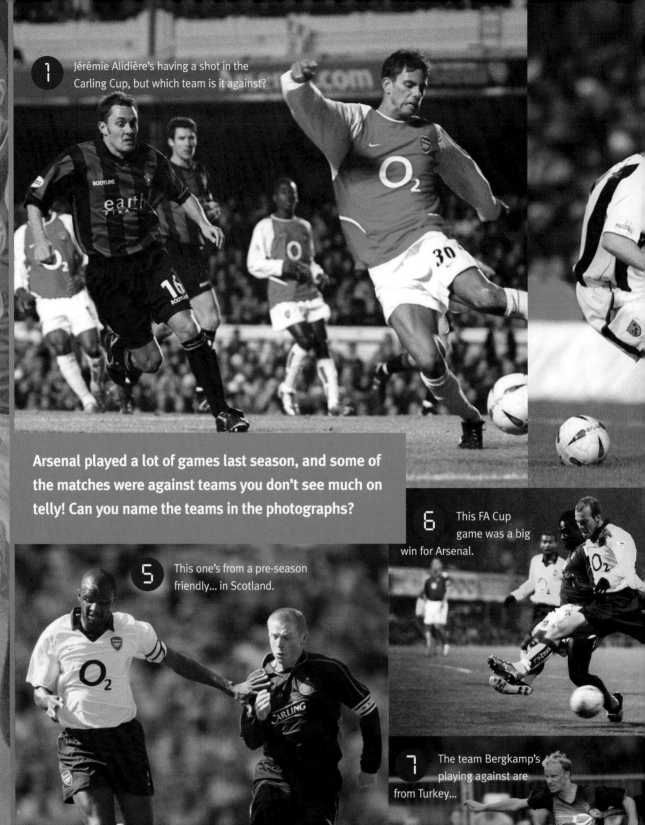

1 Jérémie Alidière's having a shot in the Carling Cup, but which team is it against?

Arsenal played a lot of games last season, and some of the matches were against teams you don't see much on telly! Can you name the teams in the photographs?

5 This one's from a pre-season friendly... in Scotland.

6 This FA Cup game was a big win for Arsenal.

7 The team Bergkamp's playing against are from Turkey...

2 Edu's playing against a First Division team. Can you name it?

3 Arsenal played this team five times in the FA Cup, Carling Cup and League!

4 The opponents for this Champions League game came from a long way away!

8 This is another Champions League game, but not the group stages...

One of Arsenal's players scored a remarkable goal at the end of the season... Can you guess the player and which team he scored against? The answer's on page 61.

The Arsenal trophy room is a busy place. Not only does it include the 25 major honours we've won during our history, it also includes all sorts of weird and wonderful treasures that have been donated to the Club throughout its history. Take a look, then, at some of the treasures of Highbury.

The League... (A)

The Premiership trophy has had three separate arrivals in the Highbury trophy cabinet – in 1998, 2002 and 2004. The trophy itself weighs over three stone. Fans have queued up to have their photo taken with this famous piece of silverware, and have their own piece of history!

Norway No Way! (B)

In 1937, an England team including three Arsenal stars played a friendly in Norway and won 6–0. Over 70 years later, the ball used in that game is still in the Arsenal trophy cabinet. It was donated by the family of one of the players, Alf Kirchen, when he passed away.

...and Cup (C)

The FA Cup trophy first entered the marble halls in 1930. It has been back eight times since.

Branching Out (D)

In 2001, Arsenal's Champions League opponents Real Mallorca donated this Mallorcan figure (left) trophy to Arsenal. Just weeks later, the Greek side Panathinaikos donated a silver olive branch mounted on a wooden base (right). The image of the olive branch represents the city of Athens and its sporting traditions.

Eastern Promise (E)

In 1981, Arsenal played a post-season friendly against Eastern in Hong Kong. They were presented with this 50cm high trophy after winning 3–0. Made of tin, it also has a red, white and blue ribbon.

Dream Team

Over the past few years, over 50 former Arsenal players have been asked to name their Arsenal All Time XI. The results have been compiled and here is the ULTIMATE Arsenal team – as voted for by many of the stars who have played for Arsenal.

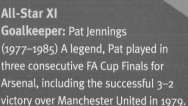

All-Star XI

Goalkeeper: Pat Jennings (1977–1985) A legend, Pat played in three consecutive FA Cup Finals for Arsenal, including the successful 3–2 victory over Manchester United in 1979.

Left-back: Kenny Sansom (1980–1989) Kenny was a committed captain at Highbury and led Arsenal (as well as England) to a host of terrific victories.

Centre-back: Tony Adams (1983–2002) Kenny's successor as captain, Adams became Arsenal's youngest captain when he took the armband. He won a host of trophies at Highbury including four League titles before he retired.

Centre-back: Frank McLintock (1964–1973) The captain of the 1971 Double-winning side, 'Big' Frank was superb in the heat of the battle and set the standard for future Arsenal captains.

Right-back: Lee Dixon (1988–2002) Lee won two Doubles and four League titles in total at Arsenal. He was part of the famous back four that emerged under George Graham's managerial reign.

Midfielder: Robert Pires (2000–present) A key component of Arsenal's 2002 and 2004 title-winning campaigns, Robert's skill and pace have won him admirers across the world.

Midfielder: Patrick Vieira (1996–present) Another player to have worn the captain's armband, Patrick continues to lead Arsenal to trophy after trophy.

Midfielder: Liam Brady (1973–1980) Star of Arsenal's 1979 FA Cup Final victory over Manchester United, Liam is one of the most naturally talented players to grace the Highbury turf. He currently heads the Arsenal Youth Development.

Midfielder: George Armstrong (1961–1977) Known as 'Geordie', Armstrong was an effective and legendary wide-player for the Gunners and part of the 1971 Double team.

Striker: Ian Wright (1991–1998) Currently Arsenal's greatest ever goalscorer, Wrighty scored 185 goals and won the Premiership, FA Cup and League Cup at Highbury.

Striker: Thierry Henry (1999–present) Closing in on Ian Wright's record, Thierry Henry has already won two Premiership trophies and the FA Cup twice while at Arsenal.

The panel that voted for the above team included over 50 former Arsenal stars, including Bob Wilson, Nigel Winterburn, Charlie George, Alan Smith, Michael Thomas and Frank McLintock.

The Wenger Era Dream Team

Such has been the success under Arsène Wenger that you could name several dream teams out of the players the French genius has fielded over the past eight years. Here is the pick of Wenger's wonderlads! See if you agree with our selection...

Goalkeeper: David Seaman
Defender: Lauren, Tony Adams, Sol Campbell, Ashley Cole
Midfielders: Robert Pires, Patrick Vieira, Emmanuel Petit, Marc Overmars
Strikers: Thierry Henry, Dennis Bergkamp

2003

Left to right: Celebrations at White Hart Lane, Gilberto's first goal at Highbury, Arsène Wenger's 400th match for the Gunners, Fabregas becomes the Club's ever youngest goalscorer.

Sunday August 16, 2003
Arsenal 2–1 Everton,
Premiership

Arsenal won on their opening matchday for the third year running.

Sunday August 24, 2003
Middlesbrough 0–4 Arsenal,
Premiership

Sol Campbell was key in keeping a clean sheet for Arsenal in this, his 100th game for the Club. Sol originally made his debut for Arsenal at the Riverside against Middlesbrough on August 18, 2001.

Friday September 26, 2003
Arsenal 3–2 Newcastle United,
Premiership

Brazilian World Cup winner Gilberto scores his first goal at Highbury.

Saturday October 4, 2003
Liverpool 1–2 Arsenal,
Premiership

This was Arsenal's seventh match in a row unbeaten against Liverpool.

The longer the season went on, the more records Arsenal shattered. The statisticians had a field day as Arsenal set and broke record after record in a memorable campaign. Of course, the only thing on the minds of the Arsenal team throughout the season was that they wanted to win every match. But now the campaign is over, we can all sit back and recall a season of memorable milestones and hit records...

Arsenal

Saturday November 22, 2003
Arsenal 3–0 Birmingham City, Premiership

This was Arsène Wenger's 400th match in charge of Arsenal and Robert Pires scored the 500th Arsenal Premiership strike in the same match.

Tuesday November 25, 2003
Inter Milan 1–5 Arsenal, Champions League

This superb victory was Arsenal's biggest ever winning margin in the Champions League.

Tuesday December 2, 2003
Arsenal 5–1 Wolverhampton Wanderers, Carling Cup

Francesc Fabregas became Arsenal's youngest ever goalscorer at 16 years and 212 days.

Left to right: Champions League action against Celta Vigo, Premiership action against Manchester United, Arsenal Ladies team celebrate on the streets of Islington.

Arsenal

Tuesday February 10, 2004
Arsenal 2–0 Southampton,
Premiership

Thierry Henry scores his 100th Premiership goal for Arsenal

Sunday February 15, 2004
Arsenal 2–1 Chelsea,
FA Cup

This match was Arsenal's 16th consecutive FA Cup round win and meant they had beaten Chelsea in the FA Cup for the fourth consecutive year.

Tuesday February 24, 2004
Celta Vigo 2–3 Arsenal,
Champions League

Edu's spectacular first goal of the evening was Arsenal's 100th in the Champions League. It had taken 67 games for the Club to reach this century.

Saturday February 28, 2004
Arsenal 2–1 Charlton Athletic,
Premiership

The day Charlton visited Highbury was the 300th day since Arsenal last lost in the Premiership. Robert Pires scored his 50th goal for Arsenal.

Saturday March 20, 2004
Arsenal 2–1 Bolton,
Premiership

Arsenal broke their own record for the longest unbeaten Premiership sequence. That 31-match sequence began at the tail-end of the 2002–2003 season. The previous Arsenal record unbeaten Premiership run was of 30 games – from December 18, 2001 to October 19, 2002.

The victory over Bolton also equalled the longest unbeaten start to a League season, previously set by Leeds and Liverpool. Leeds set the record in the 1973–1974 season and a Kenny Dalglish-inspired Liverpool equalled it in the 1987–1988 season.

2004

Sunday March 28, 2004
Arsenal 1–1 Manchester United,
Premiership

Way back in the 1920–1921 season,
Burnley remained unbeaten for 30
matches. Arsenal matched that
record with this 1–1 draw with
Manchester United.

When Thierry Henry netted a wonder
goal against United, he equalled
Arsenal's Premiership goalscoring
record. Ian Wright scored 104 goals in
191 Premiership games for Arsenal.
Thierry scored 104 goals in 164
Premiership appearances.

Saturday April 3
Arsenal 0–1 Manchester United,
FA Cup

This tie meant Arsenal had appeared in
more FA Cup Semi-Finals than any other
team in the history of football. It was
their 24th FA Cup Semi-Final. It brought
to an end a 19-match unbeaten run in
the FA Cup.

Friday April 16, 2004
Arsenal 5–0 Leeds United,
Premiership

Thierry Henry scored four goals,
his fourth marking his 150th goal
for the Club.

Sunday April 25, 2004
Tottenham Hotspur 2–2 Arsenal,
Premiership

The Gunners win the Premiership title
and Arsène Wenger becomes the first
Arsenal manager to steer the Club to
three League titles.

Monday May 3, 2004
Arsenal Ladies 3–0 Charlton Athletic
FA Cup Final

Vic Akers led his team to their sixth
successful cup final, meaning he has
a 100 per cent record in the oldest cup
competition's last stage. The Ladies
went on to win the League too – for
another Double!

GUNNERSAURUS

IN
THE BIG PARADE

I'D BETTER GET UP! I'VE GOT A BIG DAY TODAY READERS - YIPPEE!!

MMM, MMMM, MM, MMMMM, MMM

I'M REALLY LOOKING FORWARD TO THE OPEN TOP BUS PARADE TODAY.

OOPS! WHERE IS MY TICKET?

MUM, HAVE YOU SEEN MY TICKET?

WHAT TICKET?

MY TICKET FOR THE PARADE!

I DIDN'T KNOW YOU HAD ONE, DEAR.

OH NO! WHAT HAVE I DONE WITH MY TICKET?

I'M OFF TO LOOK FOR MY TICKET.

GUNNERSAURUS HAS A LOOK ON THE PITCH...

NOTHING HERE.

... AT THE TICKET OFFICE...

DARREN, HAVE YOU SEEN MY TICKET?

SORRY GUNNNERSAURUS, WE HAVEN'T.

... DON'T FORGET TO CHECK OUT THE JUNIOR GUNNERS INFORMATION ON PAGE 7!

WHERE DO YOU THINK THE BALL IS – A, B, C OR D?

SEE IF YOU CAN SPOT THE 8 DIFFERENCES BETWEEN THE TWO PHOTOS

Freddie Ljungberg

An energetic, big game player, Freddie's star just won't stop rising as he continues to perform superbly on the pitch and becomes increasingly celebrated off it!

The Lowdown: When Freddie first stepped onto the Highbury turf as a late substitute against Manchester United in 1998, far from slowly finding his feet, he chipped a delightful goal to seal a 3–1 victory. He hasn't looked back since. Winning two League championships and two FA Cups.

Freddie combines a superb engine with an expert sense of timing – two qualities that have seen him score a number of important goals from midfield. So often, his goals come in the games that matter – championship matches during the run-in or big Champions League ties such as the 5–1 defeat of Inter Milan.

The Swedish international was the Barclaycard Player of the Season in 2002 and was included in the Premier League Overseas Team of the Decade. Freddie has also attracted attention off the pitch for his stylish dress-sense and budding modelling career.

An absolute fans' favourite, in the past the Highbury faithful have sung "We love you Freddie, cos you've got red hair". But the truth is, this all-action hero would be a favourite of the fans whatever colour his hair is.

Season highlight:
His goal in the 2–1 home win over Tottenham Hotspur in November.

Patrick Vieira says:
"Freddie has an incredible engine and a good heart. His contribution to our successes cannot be over-estimated. He scores important goals but there is so much more than that to his game."

Arsène Wenger says:
"He has amazing technique and is a very talented player. He's been popular at Highbury since he first joined and I think everyone can see now that Freddie is an exceptional player."

Freddie says:
"I enjoy the football here in England because it encourages attacking play."

NAME	FREDDIE LJUNGBERG
BORN	APRIL 16, 1977 VITTSJO, SWEDEN
POSITION	MIDFIELDER
HEIGHT	176CM
WEIGHT	75KG
PREVIOUS CLUBS	HALMSTADS (SWE)

Watching the versatile Kolo develop as a centre-back was one of the joys of last season for all Arsenal fans. Having won his first Championship medal, Kolo has a very bright future ahead of him!

The lowdown: During his first full season at Highbury, Kolo played mostly at right-back or in midfield and only occasionally played at centre-back. His first goal came during a super-sub appearance at Stamford Bridge, saving a point in the 1–1 draw. In the title-winning 2003–04 season, Kolo moved full-time to a new position (familiar to him at international level) and absolutely blossomed playing in the centre of defence, alongside Sol Campbell. A popular, wholehearted player, Kolo won praise across Europe for his assured displays in all competitions. It was hard to believe this was his first season in the Premiership as a centre-back – he played like an experienced veteran!

Kolo Toure

KOLO TOURE	NAME
MARCH 19, 1981 IN IVORY COAST	BORN
DEFENDER	POSITION
183CM	HEIGHT
76KG	WEIGHT
ASEC MIMOSAS (IVO)	PREVIOUS CLUB

Kolo has now won the FA Cup (and few will forget his Millennium Stadium acrobatic flip during the celebrations that followed the 1–0 victory over Southampton and now the Premiership. He has also won a regular place in the Ivory Coast national side.

But most of all, he has captured the imagination and won the hearts of the Highbury faithful. Here's to a long, successful Arsenal career for Kolo!

Season highlight:
His solid performance in the San Siro as Arsenal beat Inter Milan 5–1.

Patrick Vieira says:
"Last year he was playing at right-back or in midfield, but I think centre-back is his real position and he's really enjoying his football. Kolo is one of those guys who just loves the game."

Arsène Wenger says:
"Kolo has settled into a centre-half position and that's where I see his future at the Club. He has done fantastically well this season."

Kolo says:
"When I play I want to give as much for the fans as I possibly can and I am so pleased if I do well. I hope that makes the supporters happy. It makes me really happy when I see supporters smiling. I am still young and learning as a player. I can get better and hopefully that will keep people happy with the way I play for Arsenal."

As the established stars of the first-team continued to shine in stadiums across the country, a second-string of promising Arsenal starlets continued to emerge into first-team reckoning during the 2003–04 season. Here's your chance to get to know five of the best!

NAME GRAHAM STACK

POSITION GOALKEEPER

The Lowdown: After five years in the Arsenal youth system, 'Stacky' was given his first squad number for the 2003–04 season. A regular for the Republic of Ireland Under-21 national team, he also had a spell in the Belgian League. A promising keeper, Stacky will go far.

NAME FRANCESC FABREGAS

POSITION MIDFIELDER

The Lowdown: 'Cesc' exploded onto the scene with a goal against Wolves in the Carling Cup (see opposite). Considered one of Spain's hottest young prospects, he moved from the Barcelona academy to join Arsenal. A lively and exciting player, he looks set to have a big future at Highbury.

NAME GAEL CLICHY

POSITION DEFENDER

The Lowdown: This promising French defender joined from Cannes, Patrick Vieira's old club, and made a number of solid performances for the first-team during the 2003–04 season. Great pace, agility and awareness make Gael a special talent.

NAME DAVID BENTLEY

POSITION MIDFIELDER/STRIKER

The Lowdown: He's been compared with Dennis Bergkamp – and not just because they share the same initials! David is a talented and committed star with great skill who has already made some promising appearances for the first-team – and let's not forget the wonder-goal against Middlesbrough in the FA Cup Fourth Round.

NAME JEREMIE ALIADIERE

POSITION STRIKER

The Lowdown: A pacey striker, Jérémie has overcome bad luck with injury to keep a high profile at Arsenal. He is a graduate of the Clarefontaine Academy in France, along with Nicolas Anelka and Thierry Henry. Jérémie has already got a number of first-team performances and goals under his belt – here's to many more in the future!

There was never a dull moment during Arsenal's Carling Cup campaign. An epic penalty shoot-out, a glimpse into the future with the emergence of a number of exciting new talents and yet more games against Middlesbrough – the cup gave Gunners fans plenty of reasons to be cheerful!

Left: Frankie Simek.
Right: Fabregas becomes the Club's youngest-ever scorer.

Sylvain's Shoot-out

With the score at 1–1 after 120 minutes of football at Highbury, a young Arsenal side and Rotherham United needed a penalty shoot-out to separate them. Shoot-outs are usually tense affairs but who would have guessed that each side would take 11 penalties before the tie was settled? Eventually Sylvain Wiltord – with his second penalty of the shoot-out – settled the tie 9–8 on penalties. Dramatic stuff!

The Youngest Gun

When young Jérémie Aliadière struck twice against Wolves in the 5–1 victory at Highbury, the young Frenchman was one of the most experienced players on the pitch! Spanish midfielder 'Cesc' Fabregas – who in the previous round against Rotherham United had become the youngest player ever to appear for Arsenal at the tender age of 16 years and 177 days – capped the night with a simple goal that made him Arsenal's youngest-ever goalscorer. Kanu and Wiltord also netted.

Future Perfect?

Throughout the Carling Cup run, Arsenal's second string showed that they could more than hold their own against the first-teams from other top clubs. Arsenal fans were treated to a tantalising glimpse of the fruits that the Club's Youth Academy is producing. Against Rotherham United there were debuts for David Bentley – who was to score his first goal for Arsenal within weeks – and the American Frankie Simek. Gael Clichy also had a run-out in the Carling Cup and the experience he picked up served him well when he was called once again into the first-team during the closing stages of the Championship race.

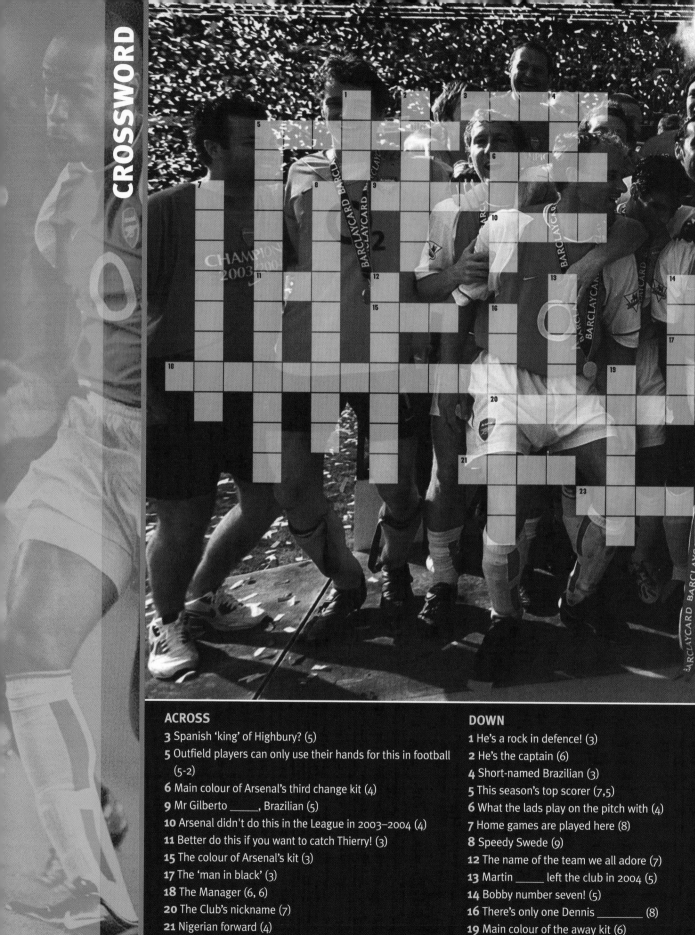

ACROSS

3 Spanish 'king' of Highbury? (5)

5 Outfield players can only use their hands for this in football (5-2)

6 Main colour of Arsenal's third change kit (4)

9 Mr Gilberto _____, Brazilian (5)

10 Arsenal didn't do this in the League in 2003–2004 (4)

11 Better do this if you want to catch Thierry! (3)

15 The colour of Arsenal's kit (3)

17 The 'man in black' (3)

18 The Manager (6, 6)

20 The Club's nickname (7)

21 Nigerian forward (4)

23 Defender from the Ivory Coast (6)

DOWN

1 He's a rock in defence! (3)

2 He's the captain (6)

4 Short-named Brazilian (3)

5 This season's top scorer (7,5)

6 What the lads play on the pitch with (4)

7 Home games are played here (8)

8 Speedy Swede (9)

12 The name of the team we all adore (7)

13 Martin _____ left the club in 2004 (5)

14 Bobby number seven! (5)

16 There's only one Dennis _____ (8)

19 Main colour of the away kit (6)

22 Also known as the 'onion bag' (3)

A	F	T	N	B	X	Y	U	I	O	L	H	S
S	G	Y	H	W	N	U	D	W	C	O	Z	E
U	P	A	Q	I	F	I	E	E	J	E	X	Y
N	M	H	E	C	E	B	A	O	L	O	S	E
B	A	R	P	H	I	R	B	J	J	Q	E	R
E	K	M	R	E	U	E	R	D	U	R	H	O
A	G	N	E	L	X	D	E	Y	N	U	J	I
T	R	O	D	S	A	C	G	K	G	O	E	N
E	E	R	P	E	E	F	N	T	B	L	S	O
N	B	T	L	A	U	R	E	N	E	R	E	T
W	S	H	E	P	T	D	W	K	R	A	R	N
I	I	B	S	D	E	R	W	A	G	P	I	A
Z	N	A	A	P	W	I	I	F	T	Y	P	E
A	N	N	E	V	B	E	R	C	R	A	F	S
L	E	K	V	B	D	S	H	T	K	R	E	O
O	D	V	S	N	O	I	P	M	A	H	C	J

There's a lot going on in this Wordsearch puzzle. Can you find all the words that relate to Arsenal's fantastic record-breaking season? Here are some clues to help you...

Q. Arsenal didn't _____ a single League game – they went through the season _____.

Q. There's only one _____ _____

Q. It is now called the North Stand, but used to be called the _____ ____

Q. We beat this team 2–1 twice in one week!

Q. A right-back from Cameroon: _____

Q. The captain's first name: _____

Q. Arsène _____ is the manager.

Q. We are the _____!

Q. Freddie _____ roams the midfield!

Q. Also known as the Romford Pele: ___ _____

Q. A Spanish signing from Seville: ____ _____ ____

Q. Robert _____ scored more goals than anyone else this season, apart from Henry.

Q. He wears the number 14 shirt: _____ Henry

Q. Brazilian with a three-letter surname: ___

Thierry Henry scores a lot of goals, and so does Robert Pires. But there are some Arsenal players who don't score much – mainly because they are running the midfield, defending or sitting in goal. Here are a few goals from the unusual suspects!

Arsenal

1) Sol Campbell doesn't just head the ball away from his goal – sometimes he heads it into the opposition's! Here is Sol scoring against Aston Villa in August.

2) Francesc Fabregas hasn't played much yet, but when he does he looks great: he was superb for the team this season, particularly in the Carling Cup. Here he is getting a goal against Wolverhampton Wanderers.

3) As well as being a great defender, Kolo Touré makes the odd run upfield to try for a goal. This one came against Wolves at Molineux in February.

4) He's the captain and he's a rock in midfield, but Patrick Vieira is good for a few goals every season. This time Chelsea were on the receiving end.

5) This one's a bit of a cheat to be honest, but we though you might like to see a goalie scoring! Here, Graham Stack nets one in the Carling Cup penalty shoot-out against Rotherham United.

Arsenal Quiz

1 Southampton. 2 Thierry Henry.
3 Chelsea. 4 Ashley Cole.
5 Middlesbrough. 6 Chelsea.
7 Thierry Henry, against Everton.
8 Middlesbrough. 9 Robert Pires.
10 Thierry Henry. 11 Juventus.
12 Giovanni van Bronckhorst.
13 Jose Antonio Reyes.
14 False, he joined from Marseille.
15 2000. 16 Borussia Dortmund.
17 Corinthians. 18 Leeds United.
19 Barcelona. 20 False, he signed from
Aletico Mineiro.
21 Birmingham City.
22 Internazionale Milan.
23 Ivory Coast. 24 1999–2000.
25 Freddie Ljungberg.
26 Cameroon. 27 Man United.
28 Monaco. 29 French. 30 Martin Keown. 31 False, he has over 15
caps. 32 Dennis Bergkamp. 33 Sylvain Wiltord. 34 Two. 35 Nigeria.
36 Sweden. 37 Thierry Henry. 38 Gilberto. 39 Republic
of Ireland. 40 David Bentley. 41 Freddie Ljungberg.
42 Honorary OBE. 43 Thierry Henry. 44 Horse. 45 Dennis
Bergkamp. 46 Robert Pires. 47 Teddy Sheringham.
48 Singing carols. 49 Sol Campbell. 50 Robert Pires.

Crossword

Wordsearch

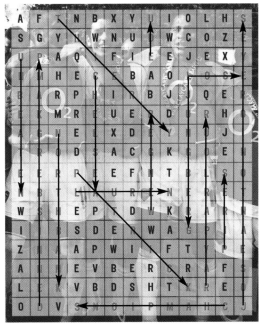

Spot the Ball

1 B. 2 B.

Spot the Difference

Guess the Team

1 Rotherham United. 2 West Bromwich
Albion. 3 Middlesbrough. 4 Lokomotiv
Moscow. 5 Glasgow Celtic.
6 Portsmouth. 7 Besiktas. 8 Celta Vigo.

Guess the Player

Jose Antonio Reyes (against Fulham).